W9-COJ-796

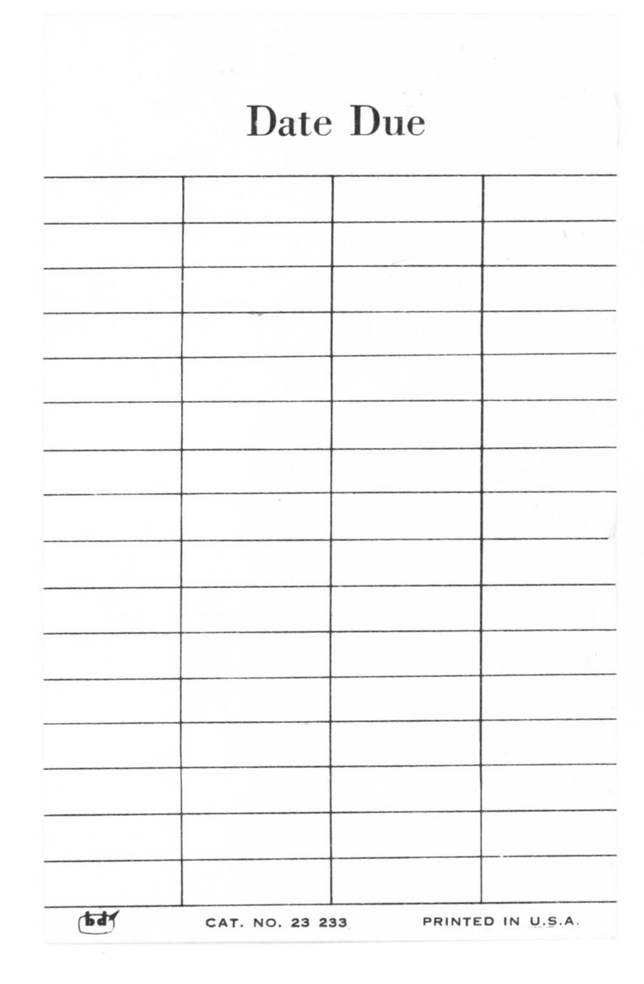
Date Due
CAT. NO. 23 233
PRINTED IN U.S.A.

Designed by Walter Swartz.
Production Coordination by Mary Greve.
Editorial Direction by Barbara Eddins.
Photography Design and Direction by David Strout.
Photographed by Keith Carey and Bill Franklin.

Set in Janson, a typeface designed by Nicholas Kis in 1690.

Printed in the United States of America.
Library of Congress Catalog Card Number: 76-418
Standard Book Number: 87529-504-5

Jerry Smith's Collections from the American Past

Jerry Smith's

Wooden Marching Band, hand-carved by Earl Eyman of Drumright, Oklahoma

Collections from the American Past

Selections from more than 11,000 items — from antique toys to classic autos

by Curtiss Anderson

Published by Hallmark Cards, Inc. for Halls in Crown Center.

ON COLLECTING

Perhaps there are as many reasons for collecting as there are collectors. It's competitive to begin with. To find a rare piece, or especially one of a kind, is a matter of great pride. Some collectors are consumed entirely by the age of the object. Others collect to honor and preserve history. But the common thread through all is the sheer joy of accumulating treasures that represent the best of their kind ever produced.

This book highlights the vast and varied collections of Jerry Smith, whose thousands of toys alone have been called one of the most valuable and extensive collections in the world. Over 25 years Jerry has assembled some dazzling and often unique groupings of memorabilia.

When he started collecting there were few reference books to guide him. For the first ten years he relied on memory, instinct—and an old Sears & Roebuck catalog. "I don't consider myself a connoisseur," Jerry says. "Most collectors specialize, but I'm just a ragpicker who happens to love the good, square, honest look of old things."

Some ragpicker! He can identify the period, maker and relative value of almost any antique toy at a glance. Jerry feels he developed an eye for quality through osmosis. And if persistence is the name of the game, he's a winner. He recently found a rare cast-iron taxi sign that he'd been after for 25 years. In a catalog, he saw a cigar-store Indian called *The Hunter* that was a minor masterpiece. He finally located one that was garishly painted over. He removed the paint himself and discovered he had the only one of its kind to exist in a private collection.

Jerry has resisted being called the owner of his collections. He prefers guardian. This philosophy was so strongly felt that twelve years ago Jerry held the first exhibit of his collections at the Kansas City Museum. Shortly thereafter, a special Christmas exhibit was fashioned at the Hallmark Gallery in New York. Dozens of other exhibits have followed, with Jerry stipulating that the fees collected be given to help needy children.

This book, then, is dedicated to children—and the child in everyone. It is dedicated also to a simpler time when the realities of the adult world were the fantasties of the child's.

ON JERRY SMITH

Jerry Smith grew up on a prairie farm near Irish Creek, Kansas, the youngest in a family of six children. His collections today initiate from a bleak Christmas over 50 years ago when, as a six-year-old, he rifled through a Sears & Roebuck catalog, listing an array of toys for Santa Claus' urgent attention. The great day arrived, and there was only a solitary item addressed to him under the tree—a 25-cent Arcade Fordson cast-iron toy farm tractor. He blamed Santa, "the tightwad, for the skinniest Christmas I ever had."

Over the years that tractor became a pleasant obsession. And 25 years later a sister-in-law, who is an antique dealer, came across one that was identical. She presented it to Jerry along with three other antique farm toys. He then added miniatures of other farm equipment—and he was off.

By his mid-twenties, Jerry Smith was a troubled man, without direction or hope. He confronted his dilemma by taking a moral inventory of himself. His work improved, but there was still something missing. Then a man he worked for called him into his office. "He told me he had never seen a kid try so hard to get ahead," Jerry says. "But he said I was doing it all wrong. 'You don't *get* ahead, you *give* ahead,' he said. 'You give the best service and you'll get the business.' He also said that if you want happiness, there is only one way in the world to get it. You've got to *give* it."

It wasn't long before Jerry went into business for himself. And he took on "a silent partner." He turned to God, who would receive a percentage of his earnings. "I remembered a Biblical reading," Jerry says, "'What you do to the least of these, you do also to me.' So I thought I'd help those least able to help themselves. And I've had the best part of the deal ever since." Jerry annually contributes up to 30 percent of his business earnings to charity.

Jerry's philanthropy became more formalized when he started Operation Friendship to benefit unfortunate children who needed anything from special medical care to something as simple as a pair of shoes. Having three daughters himself made him even more determined to help other children. His toy collection became a natural outlet for raising funds—and Mr. Smith became a master fund raiser. When the toys are exhibited, he asks a minimum fee in four figures, half of which goes to a children's charity in the locale and half to Kansas City's Children's Mercy Hospital.

There is an especially sweet reward when the toys of yesterday's children help provide a better future for today's.

TWO GAME COMBINATION
MESSENGER BOY and CHECKERS
MOTHER GOOSE A·B·C
BOOK
SIR WALTER RALEIGH
SMOKING TOBACCO
Capacity of Factory 100 Tons Per Week
ON WRAPPER.

ON TOYS

Some collectors have been known to buy the contents of an entire house in their passion to uncover a single rare item. But more often it is a box of indiscernible odds and ends that attracts collectors—and Jerry Smith is no exception. He has waded through mountains of miscellany in search of one unusual farm toy. And many a time he'd come across an item entirely new to him that he liked simply for its shape or color or mechanics.

The age of an item holds no great significance to him. "A bad design from 1880," he says, "doesn't appeal to me as much as a good one from 1910. The oldest toy I have is Chinese from the Ming period. But it doesn't have that magnetic quality that excites me."

The toys produced 50 to 100 years ago are a remarkably accurate miniature record of civilization, ruggedly cast in precisely-formed molds. "If I want to show my grandson the way things used to be," Jerry says, "toys are the best visual record there is. And this collection tells the story of what children played with over a period of 75 years."

Toys back then were Christmas items, synonymous with Santa Claus. It wasn't until the turn of the century that they became year-round merchandise, reflecting the tastes, styles, customs and manners of their time. The range of toys, as in this collection, was awesome—hansom cabs and velocipedes, fire trucks and circus wagons, automobiles and airplanes, boats and trains, doll houses and Raggedy Anns, cap pistols and cannons, Ferris wheels and carousels, fiddling bears and jumping jacks.

Is it any wonder that a child's imagination was stirred to romantic flights of derring-do? On a single Sunday afternoon he could be Lucky Lindy or a circus clown. He could save a damsel from a raging fire or conquer a country. He could stoke a steam engine or ride in style through Central Park.

"The child is father of the man," wrote Wordsworth, and the character of children of those long-ago years was formed in part by that miniature world in the playroom. And that part of everyone will never grow up altogether.

Arcade, Model A Ford

JEWETT
KAN
109-382

2

3

4

5

1923 Jewett Touring Car *1.*
Arcade, Buick *2.*
Arcade, Reo *3.*
Kenton, Open Tourer *4.*
Arcade, Yellow Cab *5.*
Buick Coupe *6.*

6

AUTHORIZED
VALVE-IN-HEAD
Buick
MOTOR CARS
TRADE MARK REG.
SERVICE

Kilgore, Stutz Roadster

THE AUTOMOBILE

Automobiles were Jerry Smith's business as well as his pleasure. In addition to toy autos, he acquired many full-sized antique cars.

Is there anything more American than the automobile? From his early childhood, it was as much a part of Jerry Smith's growing pains as it was the country's. He was ten years old in the fall of 1927 when he saw the first Model A Ford. "And I can still see it, as plain as yesterday on the floor of the Jim Kennedy Motor Company in Frankfort, Kansas," he says. "I didn't think a more beautiful or more modern car could ever be made."

His father had a Model T that provided many a family adventure. In the winter it was often a losing battle keeping the radiator from freezing and in the summer keeping the gas tank from emptying.

The Smiths, parents and six children, devotedly attended Midnight Mass, driving across the Kansas prairie come hail or sleet or snow or rain. When the temperature went below zero, the old Model T required special attention. Jerry's father would jack up a wheel and the boys would pour scalding water in the radiator from a teakettle heated on a wood stove.

Once on their way, they'd cover the radiator to keep it from freezing before getting to town. Then they'd drain the radiator so it wouldn't freeze while they were in church. After Mass, they would repeat the same process, getting hot water wherever they could find it.

Summer picnics were occasionally eaten en route. The Model T only held a few gallons of gas and often began sputtering before reaching the station. "Once we had to push it about a quarter of a mile," Jerry says, "but it seemed more like ten miles." At every shade tree, they'd stop, eat a bit more of the picnic lunch, then push on to the station where a half-dollar's worth of gas would go a long way.

They were good times, times that are warm in Jerry's memories.

1/4
1/2
3/4
GASOLINE

Ford

JEWETT

1931 Chevrolet Deluxe Roadster

From the introduction of the first automobiles, often then called *machines*, motoring was a fashionable pastime. Essentially a luxury, the early autos sputtered and sparked down Main Street on a flamboyant Sunday drive. And holiday picnics were a much anticipated event. Entire families would pack their picnic hampers with all manner of goodies, pile into the family auto and motor about the countryside in search of the perfect spot to settle and consume the feast. The rest of the time, those automobiles were grandly pampered, resting in the stable behind the house where the family horse and carriage were kept ever at the ready. The automobile was not a dependable vehicle then, and it took some years before it was put to practical use.

The attitude toward those early cars was delightfully rendered in a diary from the 1890's. A gallant gentleman, after seeing an advertisement for an automobile, wrote the firm that his wife "liked the look of the thing." That seemed to be reason enough to order one, although he made no inquiry as to how to operate the car. He assumed from the ad that one simply got in the driver's seat, pressed a button and the vehicle carried on from there.

"I had been told in a letter from the maker," he wrote, "that to start the engine you had to turn the flywheel towards you, which I did until darkness overtook me. The only result was a pair of wornout gloves."

The gentleman's exasperation with the whole business seems evident from the fact that his wife took over the chore of reporting on the purchase she had motivated: "Tried to make our motor work. Wouldn't.... After luncheon, saw to our motor, but didn't get it out of shed ... [an engineer] spent the day on his back without results .... Motor went with benzoline for the first time. Awfully pleased....After lunch, started for home in motor-car. Had lovely drive. Awful crowd followed us. Had to beat them off with umbrella.... Police spotted us. Took our names re driving through town without red flag ahead....Proceeded to Court House — filthy place. Silly old magistrate fined us."

So much for horseless carriages.

Hayes Wichita, Gasoline Pump 1.
Children's Pedal Cars 2.-5.

1

2

3

4

5

1

HORSE AND CARRIAGE

Jerry Smith has loved horses since he was a child on a farm in Kansas, and he owns a stable full of horses today. When he started collecting, he was immediately drawn to fine toy horses and the grand variety of vehicles that they pulled. He applied the same standards judging toy horses as he did real ones. It was a two-year search before he found just the right — and rare — tallyho with four handsome horses.

"When I was a teenager I used to shuck corn with a team of horses," Jerry says. "Still, by the time I came along the romantic days of horses were over." The toy buggies were made with great precision, amazingly like their full-sized counterparts. Jerry began to add the real ones to his collection as well.

While the motor car was an instant success, it was not an instant replacement for the horse and carriage. The country doctor, for example, would never depend on anything as unreliable as an automobile in making his sick calls. The daughter of a doctor at that time noted that the family's auto was kept in an old stable where her father's faithful old horse and buggy waited ready for sick calls day and night.

Wilkins, Doctor's Spring Wagon 1.
Two-passenger Doctor's Buggy 2.
Photographed at Missouri Town 1855.

2

1

3

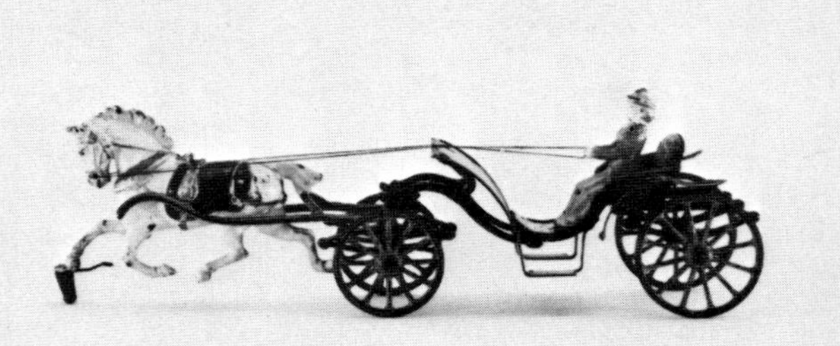

Pratt and Letchworth, Hansom Cab
Wilkins, City Truck
Wilkins, Oxford Trap
Wilkins, Horse-drawn Trolley
Wilkins, Pony Phaeton
Harness Maker's Display Horse

1
Brewster of New York, Skeleton Phaeton with C Springs 1.
Hansom Cab, Hinks & Johnson of Bridgeport 2.

Fancy rigs such as these were the ultimate status symbols of their day. But they were never seen in the rural area of Kansas where Jerry Smith grew up. "The only place I saw them as a kid was in the *National Geographic,*" Jerry says. "Even Kansas City had very few hansom cabs. Elegant carriages like these were generally found in the East, and then they belonged to people who had money." A four-passenger buggy called a rockaway was not uncommon in Kansas City, but it was never in a class with the parade of hansoms, barouches, broughams and phaetons that sallied up Fifth Avenue and through Central Park.

One of Jerry's most determined pursuits was in obtaining the hansom cab shown here. It was originally from Boston and brought to Topeka, Kansas, by two doctors. When they died, it was put up for sale. By the time Jerry caught up with it, the pristine vehicle had just been sold. He called the new owner and bought it for $600 more than it had gone for the day before.

FIRE STATION
8
8

TOYS TO FIRE THE IMAGINATION

Fire toys included a total miniaturization of the station itself with cast-iron fire wagons and horses, extension ladders and their brave attendants. The toys had superbly fashioned moving parts, simulating the real equipment.

These realistic toys gave any child of the day a sense of the real experience of fighting fires — pulling out of the station in a demonic roar, with wheels rolling across the living room floor to attack the inferno in the fireplace. And publications such as *Pluck and Luck* stirred a child's imagination with stories such as "Old Put, or the Fire Boys of Brandon":

"Old Put was first again at the scene. The mayor was on the spot seated in a carriage and watching the fire. A woman was in front of the burning building crying for her baby, which was in the building. Soon Harry Thorne was seen coming out a window with the child. He had hold of a rope and the baby was held by its dress in his teeth. Harry climbed down the rope. He swung back and forth until one of the boys caught him on the backward swing. Harry deposited the infant in its mother's arms . . . ."

Wilkins-Kingsbury, Fire Station
Wilkins, Pumper

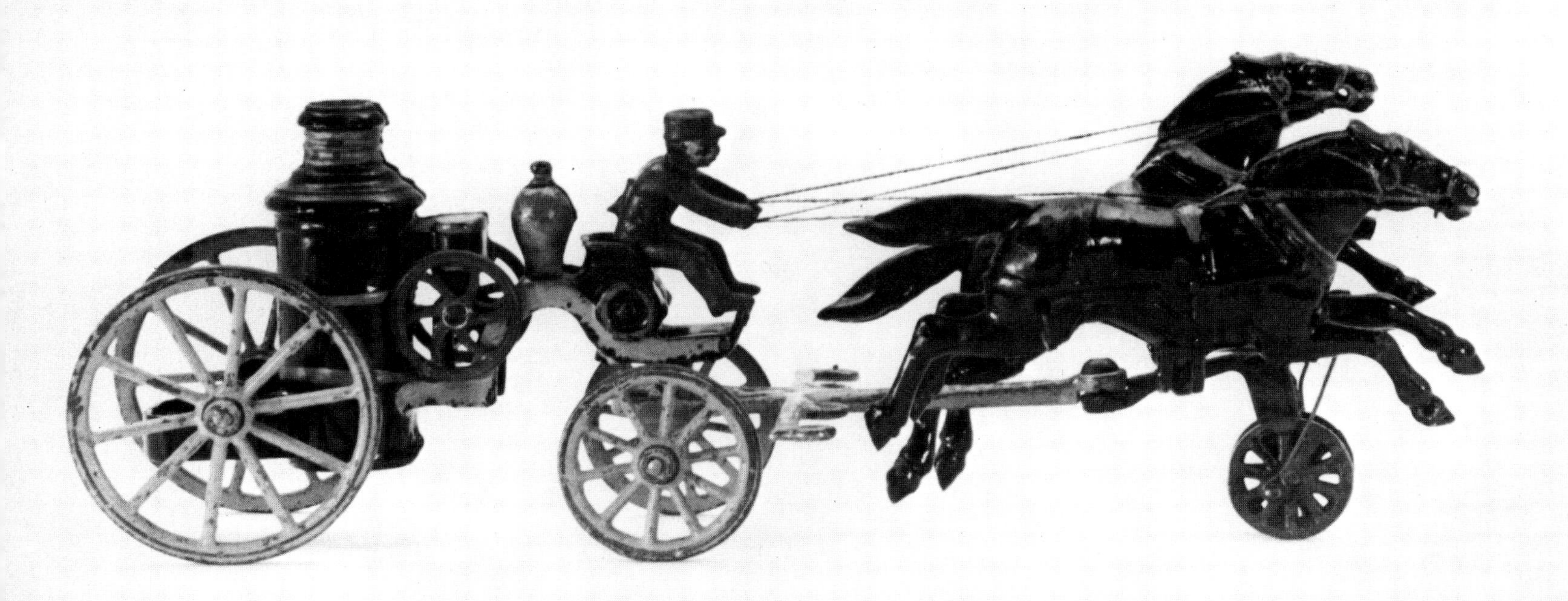

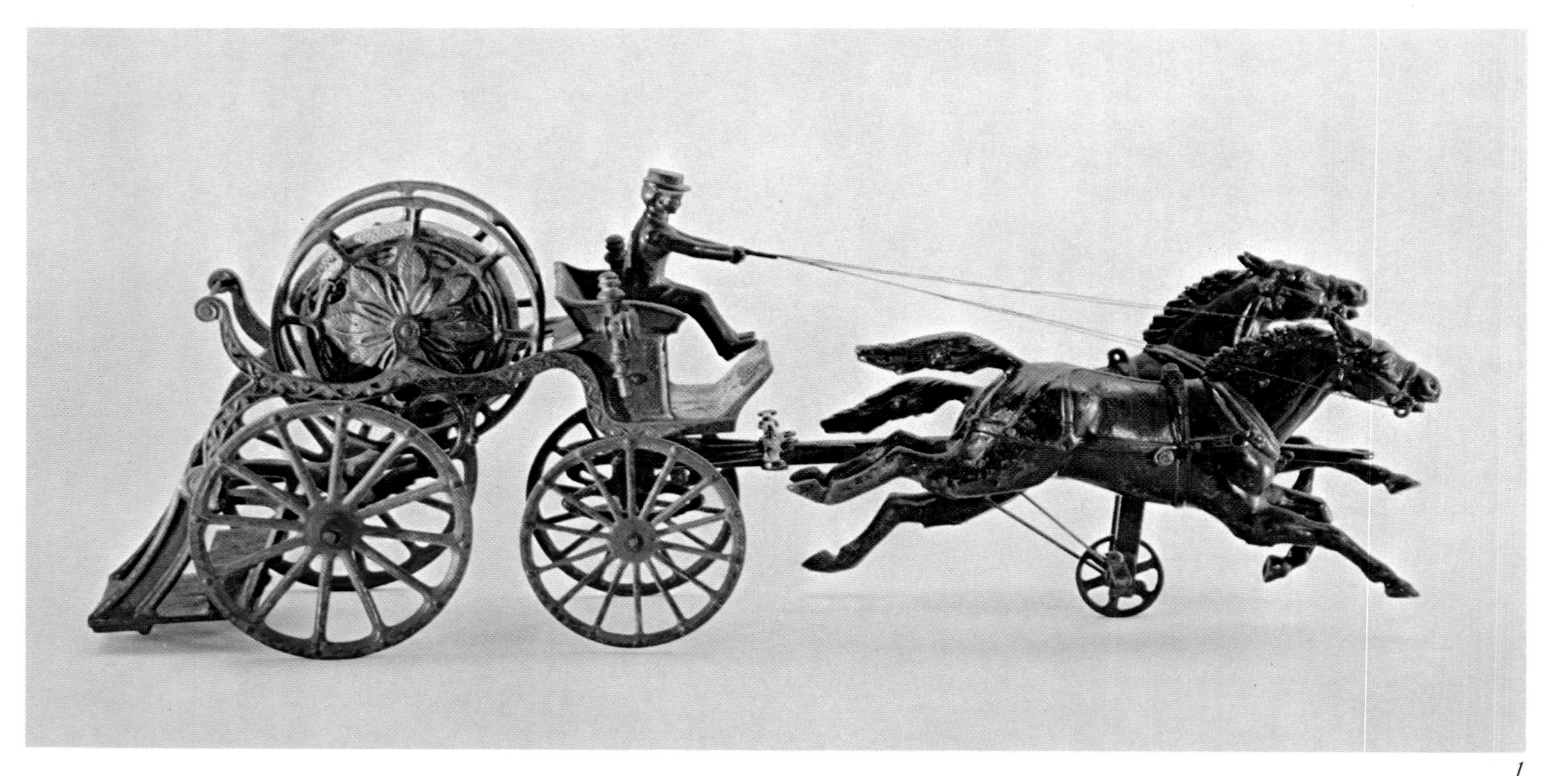

1

Ives, Giant Hose Reel 1.
Ives, Fire Patrol 2.
Wilkins, Hook and Ladder 3.
Hubley, Pumper 4.
Ives, Iron Chief Wagon 5.

What child of the 19th century didn't want to grow up to be a fireman? The range of equipment was awesome, as seen on these pages—hose wagons, fire patrols, hook-and-ladder outfits, team pumpers and chief's wagons. They looked real enough to give children a vicarious sense of control over some powerful elements of the adult world.

The horse-drawn vehicles were the first and by far the most popular. And those in cast iron seemed always the most authentic. There were also such toys in lead, tin and even wood. Few of the latter have survived.

One firm, Ives, was especially expert in producing toys of this type, and it's been reported that an Ives firehouse that sold for $10 in 1910 is worth more than $500 today.

PATROL
2
3
4

5

1

2

BELL TOY FANCIES

Children of the past loved bell toys. They rang out from an imaginary world of transportation, totally whimsical with no attempt to reflect any real-life object. Bell toys on wheels have come down through the ages to entertain children too young to manipulate miniature automobiles, trains and fire wagons.

Bell toys generally were the most ornate of all toys, with fanciful castings and details reflecting their fantasy. The bells completed the illusion, and the finest of them were toned to ring with a chime.

Monkey on Velocipede Bell Toy, J & E. Stevens Co. 1.
Two Clowns on a Donkey Bell Toy 2.
Bell Toy, George Brown 3.
Woman with Fan Bell Toy, J. & E. Stevens Co. 4.

3

4

Positively
Long Filler
Cigar 5¢
CONFECTIONERY

SIGNS OF THE PAST

Signs are one of the earliest forms of folk art. And the most interesting are those whose messages are in their shapes or symbols rather than in words — the clock, the barber pole, the eye glasses, the boot.

As Jerry Smith explains: "Early settlers who couldn't read and immigrants who didn't know the language relied on signs that identified the service offered — just as our traffic signs today speak a universal language." And, of course, these symbols were a primary form of advertising. The more extravagant ones reflected the taste and success of the merchant.

The cigar store Indian, perhaps, remains the uniquely American classic. The Kansas City Indian, on page 32 (upper right), has a tin right arm. He lost his wooden arm 70 years ago when a herd of longhorns coming down Main Street knocked it off. There were few woodcarvers around then, so the store owner had a tinsmith make him a new right arm.

1921 Ford "Model T" Depot Hack

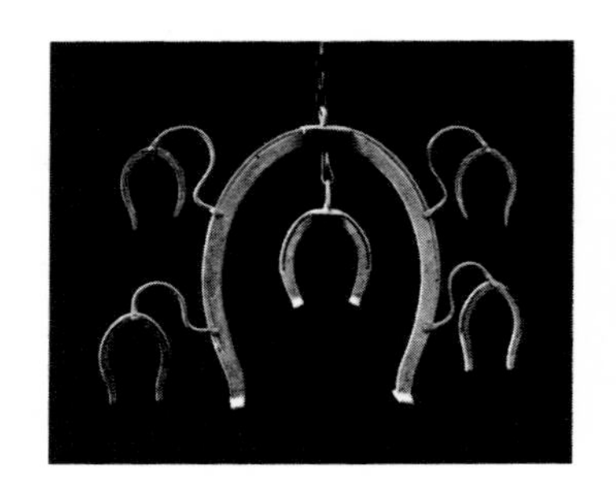

DE LAVAL CREAM SEPARATORS
THE WORLD'S STANDARD

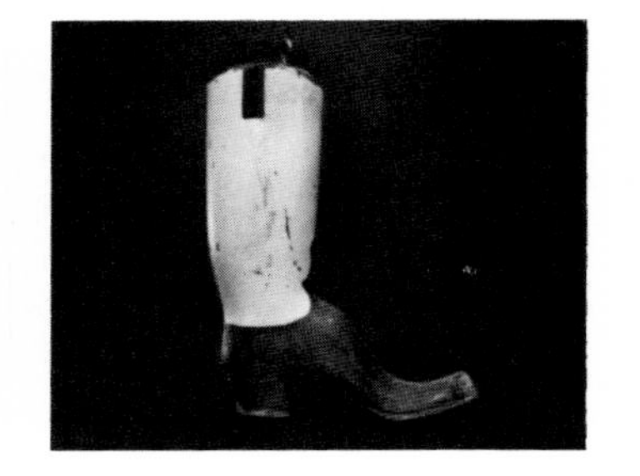

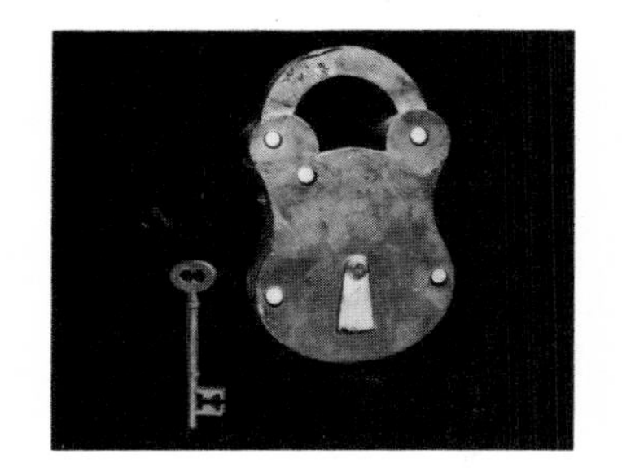

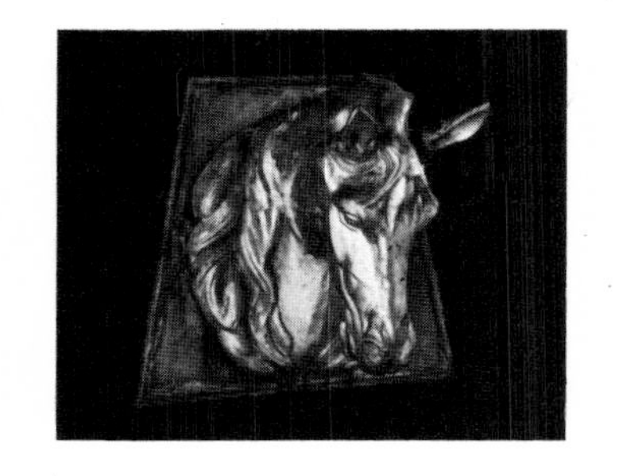

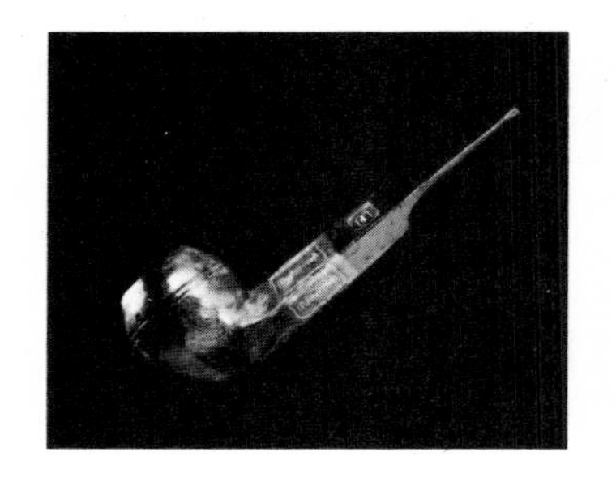

LEAVE YOUR Automobile AT
L.H.— STAHLS
TRY ONLY 10 CENTS ME
ALWAYS ROOM FOR
YOUR TEAMS

UNITED
SERVICE
MOTORS

NEW YORK CUTLERY CO

For Private Treatment of Domestic Animals
& WEBER'S

53

1

2

A CHRISTMAS VILLAGE

Christmas Village, Jerry Smith's creation, was for years a children's paradise in Kansas City—and Jerry was promptly labeled Father Christmas. He converted an old lumberyard into a festival of flower-lined streets with old-time store fronts—hardware, cobbler, blacksmith, general store. Then laden among these was his vast collection of toys and other antiques. A 1920 Nickelodeon rang out festive songs and automated elves were hard at work on new toys. Among Jerry's favorite displays—and the kids'—was an old popcorn wagon that, he says, "still makes the best popcorn in the world."

Was it all worthwhile? A resounding *yes* from Jerry. "It was the best way I could think of to share the collection. What good is it if it's just locked up somewhere where no one can see it? I was just the guardian of it. I wanted everyone to enjoy it."

The most touching testimony of all to this philosophy was a letter Jerry received from a school teacher. She had brought a small boy to the village who was confined to a wheelchair and was severely disturbed emotionally, so much so that he had not spoken a word in four years. She said that there was no physical reason for his silence. After leaving this Christmas scene, the child, apparently unable to hold back, suddenly burst out telling the teacher what he had seen—hobby horses and carriages, model houses and cars, boats and fire wagons, monkeys and rag dolls. Much to the tribute of Christmas Village, the child has been talking ever since.

Christmas Village Street 1.
Train Diorama 2.
Clockwork Santa Claus 3.

1

2

Gunterman, Mercedes, No. 50 1.
Handmade Doll House 2.
Dayton, Friction Train 3.
Tin Trolley, Hedwig Eitner, Germany 4.
Priscilla Side-paddle Wheeler, Harris Cast-iron 5.
Lehmann, Autobus 6.
Wood and Polychrome Child's Pull Toy 7.
J. & E. Stevens, Climbing Monkey, Bell Toy type 8.
American Toy Co., 8-Man Rowers 9.
Ames, Clockwork Car 10.
Papier-mache Roly-Poly 11.
Ives, Punch and Judy Cap Pistol 12.
Ives, Chinese Must-Go Cap Pistol
Ives, Sambo Cap Pistol
Carpenter, Tallyho 13.
Very early large tin Dog and Rider, George Brown 14.
The Couple Walking the Dog, Lehmann 15.
Handmade Raggedy Andy 16.
Reed, Paper Litho Cathedral 17.
Sheffield Farms Horse-drawn Wooden Milk Wagon 18.
Large Doll in Child's Stroller 19.
Early French Tin Balloon Carousel 20.
Hand-painted Noah's Ark 21.

4

5

6

7

8

9

10

1

12

13

15

16

14

17

18

19

20

21

Christmas is the season of greatest popularity for Jerry Smith and his toys. If you've ever been warmed by nostalgia while viewing a Christmas display complete with old-fashioned tree and antique dolls and rocking horses, there's a good chance that Jerry Smith was responsible. He has loaned antique toys for numerous holiday displays and exhibits where people of all ages have smiled with happy memories, inspired by a Christmas scene from out of the past.

Jerry was stunned by the response to these exhibits. The young were entertained, the middle-aged were enchanted and the elderly were sentimental. Jerry concedes the rewards of collecting are not only for children. "Older folks see some item from their youth, like the little *Ocean Queen* that reminds them of the side-wheeler ferryboats they used to ride. Then they get all misty-eyed, and darned if I don't get choked up too."

Early on Jerry saw the tapestry of history in his collection. "You can follow the development of this country through its toys," he says. "You can trace the point when people broke away from making things at home and started to accept manufactured goods. You can pinpoint the development of the steamboat, the telephone, the train, the automobile, the airplane, the introduction of electricity and even the space age. Practically every important scientific invention, historical event, lifestyle and amusement of the adult world can be seen in the toy world. Toys even reflect the changing use of materials in industry."

The riches surrounding the tree at right are a far cry from the childhood Christmas Jerry remembers. One toy farm tractor was his only gift, but it inspired an entire career of giving in years to come.

Photographed at Wornall House Museum. *1.*

O
K 5
O 6 D 6

2

WHEELER DEALERS

The bicycle, introduced in America in the late 1800's, perhaps had as much effect on social conditions as the automobile.

The sleek and fanciful vehicles began disrupting all manner of life. Employers regarded them as a curse because their owners insisted on working only 10 or 12 hours a day to give them more time to ride. Cycling on Sunday became competitive with church. And women's hemlines went up for riding comfort.

The rage finally died down a bit after there had been so many accidents on the big five-foot high-wheelers.

Child's Tricycle; Gear-driving Roadster, Springfield 1.
Stevens & Brown, Boy on Velocipede 2.
Sidesaddle Velocipede (mechanism cranks off of the handlebars) 3.
Cast-iron Boy on Tricycle, Kenton 4.

3

4

2

3

4

5

6

COMICS ON THE MOVE

Everyone looked forward to the Sunday *funnies*, or the comic strips, an event that did not escape the attention of toy manufacturers. It was free advertising for toy models of virtually every popular character—Little Orphan Annie and Sandy, Maggie and Jiggs, Felix the Cat, the Toonerville Trolley and Barney Google on Sparkplug. Every child in America wanted to own at least one of these colorful characters. Not surprisingly, many a rainy Sunday afternoon was filled with re-enactments of adventures from the pages of the morning comics.

Before long the craze also encompassed silent movie idols. Movie comics of the day enjoyed an immense following of fans, adults as well as children. Audiences shrieked and roared to the antics of Harold Lloyd hanging precariously on the hands of a skyscraper clock and Charlie Chaplin, cane and twitchy moustache, wobbling bowlegged into another lovable, laughable predicament.

The figures were ingeniously contrived wind-ups. Most of them walked. Harold Lloyd's eyes would roll. The Toonerville Trolley chugged across the floor.

These miniature representations of life's humorous aspects were enthusiastically embraced by millions of Americans.

Felix the Cat, S. Gunterman 1.
Charlie Chaplin, Early German 2.
Toonerville Trolley, Nifty 3.
Little Orphan Annie & Sandy, Marx 4.
Maggie and Jiggs, Schoenhut 5.
Harold Lloyd (Happy Fella'), Marx 6.
Barney Google on Sparkplug, Nifty 7.

1

SPAR
PLUG

ROYAL CIRCUS

Jerry Smith never saw a circus in the Kansas farming community where he grew up. However, he has more than made up for it. "Anybody who has a feel for the old days," he says, "has got to tune in on the circus wagon."

The circus parade came right through the house in lively replicas of the real event. Brightly painted cast-iron wagons were drawn by pairs of black and white horses. The giraffe wagon, shown here, is an example of a rare piece, largely because it was not a big seller in its day. The real wagons, of course, were elaborately carved of wood. At the turn of the century, when the circus was in its heyday, no event enlisted greater excitement than the circus parade.

The Humpty Dumpty Circus, on the next page, includes balance toys with slots on hands and feet so the clowns and acrobats can perform in a variety of configurations. These finely detailed toys allowed a child to re-enact every performance he had seen under the real big top.

Royal Circus Wagons, Hubley

UMPTY-DUMPTY-CIRCU

Schoenhut's Humpty Dumpty Circus

1

2

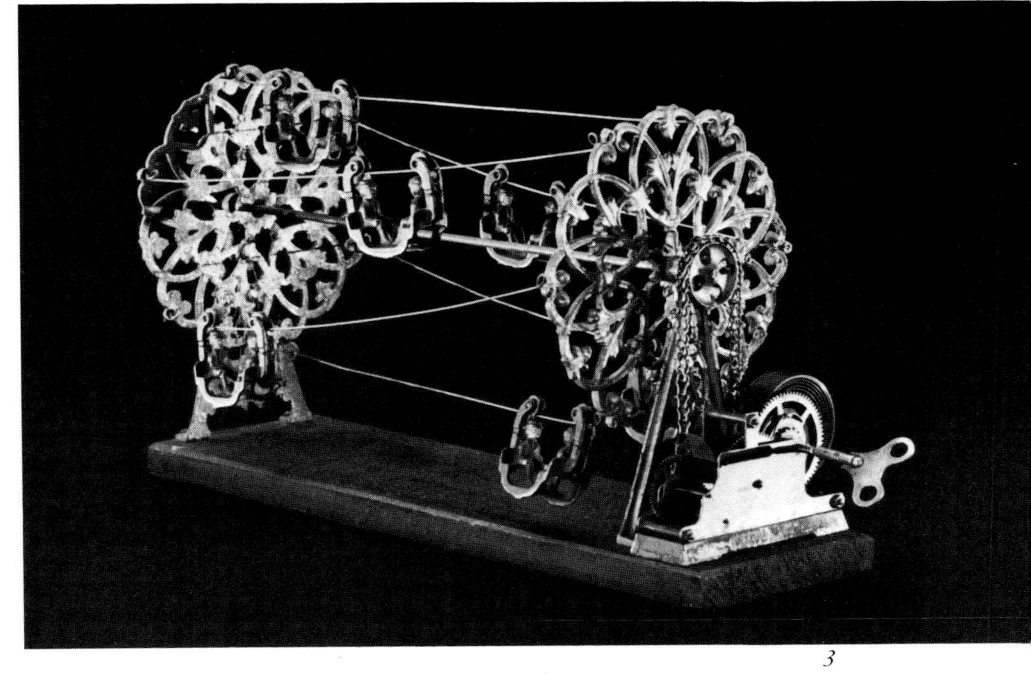

3

CLOCKWORK CARNIVAL

Along with the circus came the great white way, itself a dazzling panorama of toys.

All the carnival attractions and their attendant thrills were recreated in miniature clockwork and wind-up toys for children. They were creations of ingenuity and beauty, usually made of tin and fitted with brass works. These and all types of other mechanical scenarios brought the playroom to life. In addition to rides, like the Ferris wheel shown here from the late 19th century, there were circus figures that danced and even fiddled.

World Columbian Exhibition Ferris Wheel, Hubley 1.
Early Tin Clockwork Merry-go-round 2.
Very Early Clockwork Amusement Park Ride, Hubley 3.

1

2

3

4

PLAY AND SAVE

Banks were as clever as toys before the turn of the century. To encourage thrift, mechanical banks rewarded the child with an amusing action.

Jerry Smith describes one from his collection that borders on violence. "When you put a penny in, a globe spins, throwing a clown up into the air. It's cast iron, and if someone happens to be close to it, he could lose a few teeth."

Chief Big Moon (Indian Camp) 1.
Clown on Globe 2.
Professor Pugfrog's Great Bicycle Feat 3.
Lion and Two Monkeys 4.
Eagle and Eaglets 5.
All by J. & E. Stevens Co.

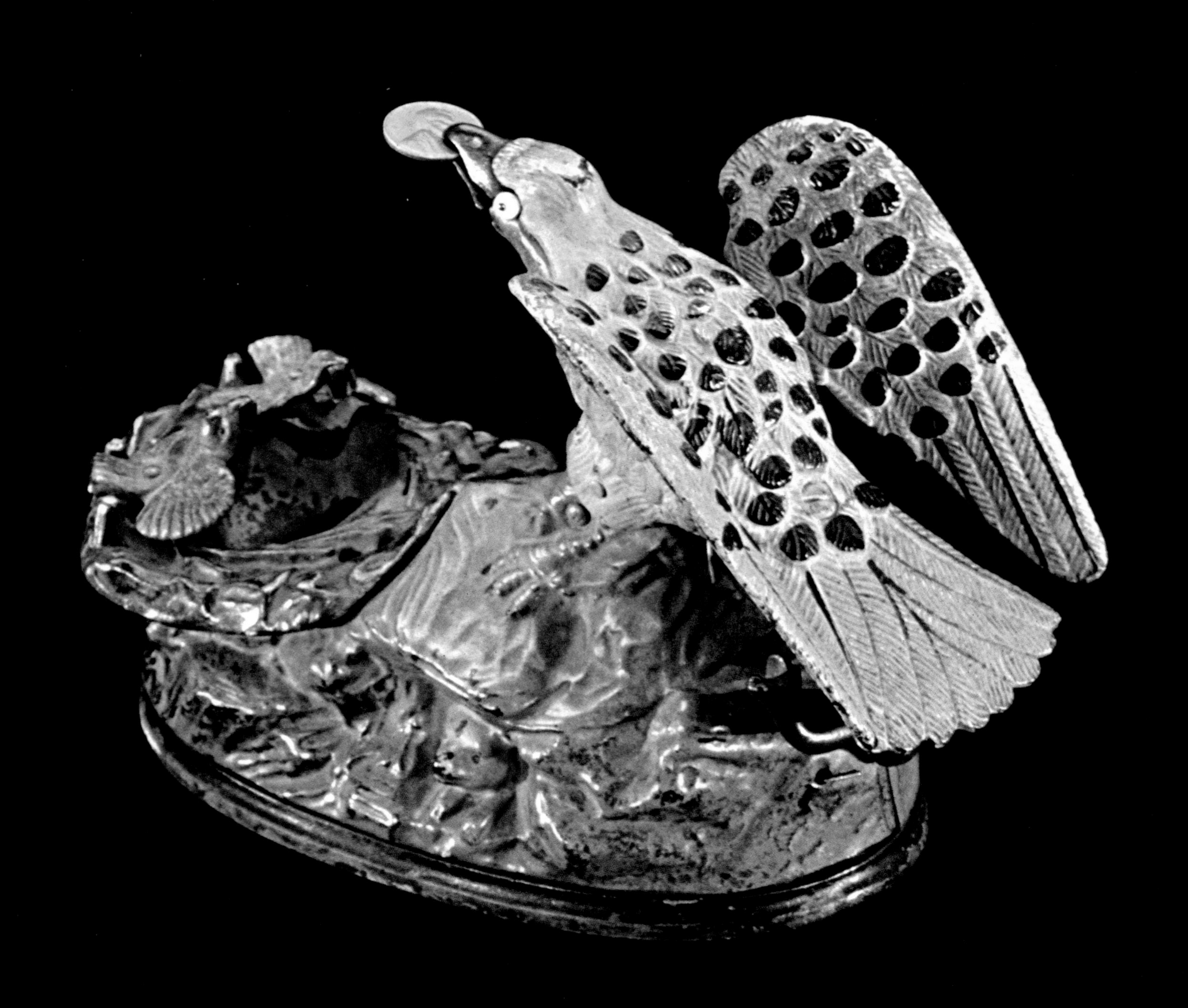

1

ALL STEAMED UP

The industrial revolution created a revolution in toymaking as well. Children learned how real things worked through their toys, especially with the advent of steam power toward the end of the 19th century.

Manufacturers produced tens of thousands of working steam toys—locomotives, trains, boats and fire engines. Even steam-powered accessories were made—grindstones, circular saws, windmills, bucket chains and pumps. Many had models of men realistically performing such tasks as sawing and blacksmithing.

They were demanding toys. Boilers had to be filled, fires fueled and steam raised. This required skill and caution. If the toy got too hot, a metal wheel could actually melt. Children learned to be careful.

The closer a child got to the reality of running a steam engine, the more he dreamed of traveling to distant places. Jerry Smith remembers: "When I was a youngster, we lived about a quarter-mile from the railroad. When I heard that train whistle, it made my blood chill. People were really going places. That old steam engine came huffing and puffing, and as a little kid, I thought the thing would blow up. And, of course, that engineer was a mighty heroic figure to me. He was in charge of a whole string of cars and that big old boiler. I think every child who grew up in my time thought the engineer of a train was almost as great a man as the President of the United States."

Gebruder Bing, Stationary Steam Plant 1.
Weeden, Live Steam Roller 2.
Marklin, Live Steam Train 3.
English Live Steam Train
Weeden, Stationary Engine with Table Saw and Drill Press Accessory 4.

2

3

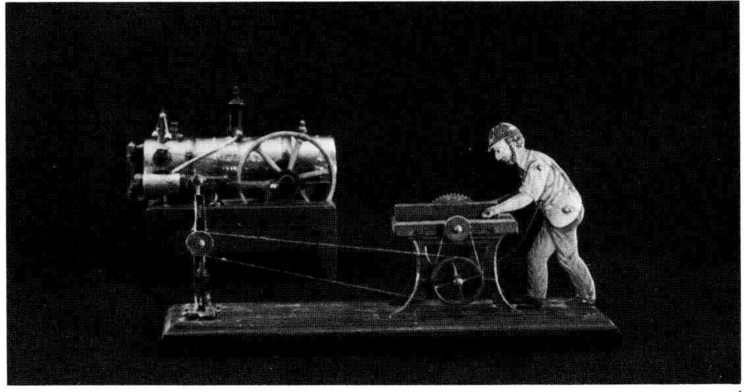

4

1

IRON HORSES

It was the railroad, of course, that opened up the country for long-distance travel, and a generation of Americans became enchanted by trains. If someone was going farther than the next town, he went by train. Toymakers were quick to recognize the appeal of miniature versions in every conceivable size, material and power of locomotion. There were tin, wood, iron and steel trains. And there were model kits of trains to be assembled by star-struck children. There were even pedal trains big enough for children to ride. There were wind-up trains, clockwork trains, steam trains and electric trains.

And children thrilled to them all, but always and especially to the full-sized locomotive that came whistling over the horizon.

Carette, Stork Leg (Live Steam) 1.
Bowman, Tank Locomotive (Live Steam)

Ives, Locomotive 2.
Ives, Locomotive
Welker & Crosby, Locomotive

2

1

2

3

Fallows, Early Tin Hand-painted Train 1.
Welker & Crosby, Iron Train 2.
Bliss, Prince Engine with Palace Coach, Paper Litho 3.
Ives, Station; Gunterman, Trolley and Trailer 4.

4

2

3

4

SHIPS AHOY!

Boats came later to Jerry Smith's collections, probably because he grew up on the Kansas prairie where the only boats he saw were in the Sears catalog.

Miniature boats at their finest can be works of art. Because of its rarity, one of Jerry's favorites is an old tin boat, the *Volunteer*, a self-propelled clockwork model from 1870. Some of the early boats were on wheels to be pulled or pushed, probably because bathtubs were not all that common in those days.

J. Falk, Tin Boat 1.
Early French Side-paddle Wheeler 2.
Marklin, Paduca 3.
Bing, Oceanliner 4.
Handmade Wood Sailing Ship Weathervane 5.

5

N
S

AMERICAN WEATHERVANES

Weathervanes and weathercocks were once synonymous, the rooster being the earliest design in this country. Eventually other farm animals and even fish and dragons appeared as weathervanes. By the 19th century, fire engines and locomotives were crafted.

Early vanes were made of wood whittled by pioneer farmers. The first metal ones were wrought iron, and later they were cut out of flat sheet metal. Eventually copper vanes came into prominence.

Weathervanes and whirligigs became symbols as much as anything. A family's status could be established by the size and complexity of the design, sometimes even identifying the type of work a man did. Today, they survive as symbols of a peaceful rural America.

Jerry Smith's collection is entirely early American. "My best one has two hackneys pulling a gig with a driver," says Jerry. "It's all done in hand-hammered copper, six-and-a-half feet long. I think it's one of a kind."

2

Full-bodied Horse Weathervane. Photographed at Missouri Town 1855 *1.*
Sheet-iron Weathervane. Photographed at Missouri Town 1855 *2.*
Folk Art Whirligig 3.
Folk Art Whirligig 4.

3

4

The Spirit of St. Louis
Builds More than
10 Different
Models
Made in St. Louis
Lindy did it!
—but more remains to be accomplished. We turn to the youth of the land for the new ideas which will place aviation on a really practical basis.
An educational toy, such as this, may prove to be the starting point for the next great development.
ST. LOUIS

1

2

3

4

FLYING HIGH

Airplanes caught the fancy of the public soon after the Wright Brothers flight. And the ever-alert toy-makers began producing models, with wind-up spring motors, that would really fly. One of the more elaborate toys was the clockwork parachute outfit at the right.

Still, flying was considered a curiosity without much of a future even after World War I. Barnstormers hit the county fair circuit, stuntmen balanced on the wings of planes and a flying circus offered rides to the public for about a dollar. It was all very whimsical.

Jerry Smith's earliest memory was of biplanes "that would never get very high and would come wobbling in for a landing that I thought they'd never make." His first plane ride was in a Ford Trimotor when he was ten years old. "It was built out of corrugated metal and looked like a flying barn," he says.

That was in 1927, a landmark year in aviation history. Lindbergh landed in Paris and air travel was to boom. President Coolidge had called him *the flying fool,* but now he was *Lucky Lindy* to everyone.

"I remember his flight like yesterday," says Jerry. "It was lunch hour at school when we got the news. What a thrill! Then there wasn't anyone greater in the world."

Countless models were made of the *The Spirit of St. Louis,* and Jerry Smith's is one of the most authentic. "Not very pretty," he says, "but it closely resembles the real plane."

Metalcraft, Airplane Kit 1.
Kingsbury, Trimotor 2.
Schieble, Friction Airplane (Hill Climber) 3.
Kingsbury, Biplane 4.
Muller & Kadeder, Clockwork Ascension and Parachute Toy 5.

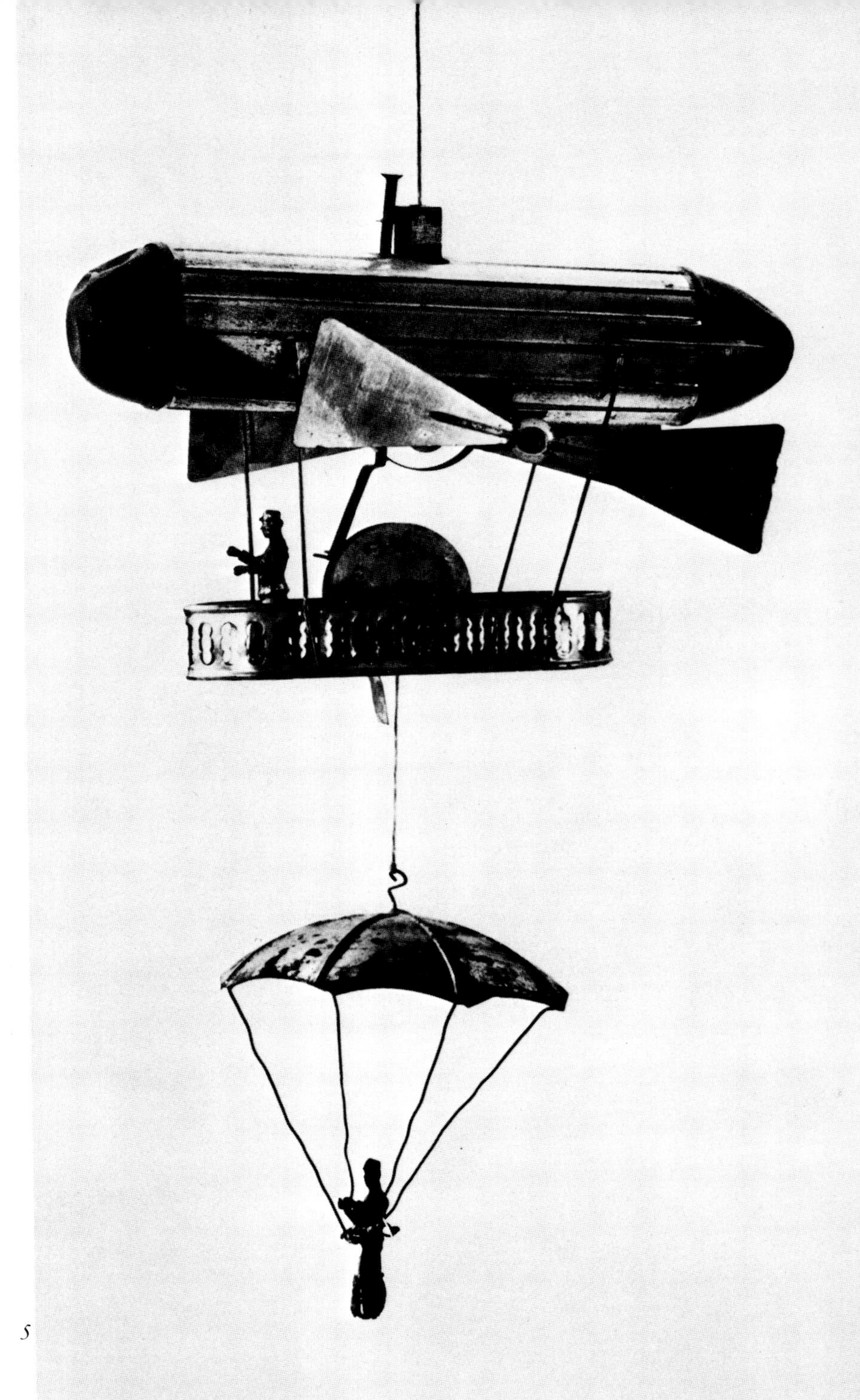

1

ALL WOUND UP

Colorful and amusing wind-up toys were the favorites of thousands of toddlers. Though they resemble clockwork toys, they were less expensive with less intricate mechanisms. Most of them were made of tin, brightly painted to complement their whimsical characters and lively movements. Those shown here are some of the best, made by Ernst Paul Lehmann in Germany. The bucking broncho does exactly what it's supposed to do, and the car and driver come with a working horn.

2

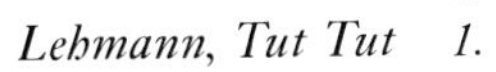

Lehmann, Tut Tut 1.
Lehmann, Anxious Bride 2.
Lehmann, Bucking Broncho 3.
Lehmann, Paddy's Dancing Pig 4.
Martin, Hindu with Mango Cart 5.

3

4

5

1
Bullrake, Early Salesman Sample *1.*
Vindex, Thresher and Tractor *2.*

JERRY SMITH, HOME AGAIN

And now it all comes back to where it began—with a simple little Arcade Fordson tractor that a six-year-old boy received some 50 Christmases ago. When he rediscovered it as a grown man, along with other farm toys made by McCormick-Deering, he recreated his own childhood in a toy world. Jerry Smith is a farm boy who came home again through his collection.

Because he had lived on a farm, these toys were the most interesting to him at the beginning of his collecting career. And memory served him well. Those pages of the Sears & Roebuck and Montgomery Ward catalogs he poured over as a child came back to mind. "We called them 'wish books' back then," Jerry recalls. "And, of course, a farm boy wanted a tractor like his dad's, and a girl wanted a little stove like her mother's."

Jerry's fondness for horses is a reversion to his youth as well. "Horses were the way you got around," he says. "And mules, too. In fact, my dad laid the name Jerry on me because I was a bulky mule myself. My name really was Aloysius, but I preferred being named after a mule to that."

There weren't many toys in the Smith household at that time, but that was true of other farm families in the area as well, so it seemed perfectly natural. Money was scarce, but again that seemed to be the condition of the whole community. Jerry's mother raised chickens to supplement the family income, "and we ate plenty of them ourselves," he adds.

"I was born at a time when I could see the old going out and new coming in," Jerry says. "A rural area, of course, was always behind the cities in the way people lived and what they owned. And in the early 1920's, we were looking at things for the first time that city folks had seen five or six years before."

He adds affectionately, "I suppose we were poor, but we never thought of it that way. We had a whale of a shortage of money, but there's a difference between that and being poor. In fact, I prefer to think of us as a depression-proof family. We worked hard, we had good health and we ate well. On a farm in those days you could be rich without money. And in a family of six children, you learn to share."

And sharing has been a motto with him ever since.

1

Wilkins, Two-mule Truck Wagon 1.
Vindex, Hayloader

The devout presence of a finely carved Amish couple 2.
raises toymaking to an art form,
representing folk art at its best.
Photographed at Missouri Town 1855.

2

Jerry Smith's Original Toy — Fordson Tractor by Arcade